TIN CAN SAILORS
SAVE THE DAY!

The USS *Johnston*
and the Battle off Samar

Kevin McDonald

PALOMA BOOKS   ASHLAND, OREGON

TIN CAN SAILORS SAVE THE DAY!
©2015 Kevin McDonald

Published by Paloma Books
(An imprint of L&R Publishing, LLC)

Paloma Books
PO Box 3531
Ashland, OR 97520
email: sales@hellgatepress.com

Editor: Harley B. Patrick
Cover Design: L. Redding
Cover Illustration: Paul Wright
Maps and Digrams: Rhys Davies (*wwwrhysspieces.com*)
(pages 12, 19, 38, 42, 48)

.

Library of Congress Cataloging-in-Publication Data available upon request

Printed and bound in the United States of America
First Edition 10 9 8 7 6 5 4 3 2 1

This book is dedicated to all the men of Taffy Three. The courage and skill they demonstrated off Samar will long be remembered as the U.S. Navy's finest hour.

CONTENTS

CHAPTER 1

Prelude

WE CAN'T GO DOWN WITH OUR FISH STILL ABOARD," said Captain Evans. "Stand by for torpedo attack."

A column of six Japanese heavy cruisers sped by on the right. Each cruiser was five times the size of Evan's ship, the destroyer USS *Johnston*. Flashes flickered from enemy guns as they fired on the *Johnston*. Some shells whistled overhead, while others crashed into the waves in front of the *Johnston*. The enemy rounds fell like rain.

Captain Evans was determined to strike back hard, and torpedoes were the *Johnston's* most powerful weapon. He chose the lead enemy ship as the target. Sailors on the torpedo mounts set the torpedoes to run at twenty-seven knots and plotted in a one-degree spread.

Evans shouted, "Fire torpedoes!"

A sailor pulled the firing lever. The first torpedo blasted out the tube, flew over the men on the rail and plunged into the water. Every three seconds another lever was pulled, launching all of the torpedoes into the deep blue sea. Ten white wakes fanned out toward the enemy cruisers.

"Fish in the water!" a sailor yelled.

On the bridge of the *Johnston* officers and sailors watched the Japanese cruiser. It disappeared into smoke and clouds off the Philippine island of Samar. One officer strained to see through the haze while another counted off the seconds to impact.

Through a gap in the clouds a geyser of water erupted beside the enemy ship. The sound of the explosion rippled across the ocean. A moment later the cruiser emerged from the haze with flames leaping from the deck. A twenty-foot section had been blown off the front of the ship.

The men on deck of the *Johnston* yelled, "Hooray!"

Their celebration was short lived. Japanese shells that had been falling around the *Johnston* finally found their mark. Three 14-inch battleship rounds pierced the thin deck armor, crushing the number two engine and knocking out all power to the rudder. The whole ship seemed to surge out of the water for a moment.

In the next moment two 6-inch rounds crashed into the *Johnston's* bridge, splintering the steel walls and cutting holes in machinery and men.

Blood poured off the bridge like water. One officer lay on the floor complaining about pain in his arms, not seeming to realize his left leg was gone below the knee. Another man was missing his head. The blast blew off two of Captain Evan's fingers.

When the ship's doctor rushed toward him, the captain waved him off. "Don't bother me now. Help some of those guys that are hurt." His shirt singed and hanging in tatters,

"Fish in the water!" Note that the photo shows a quad torpedo mount (four tubes), while each mount on the *Johnston* was a quintuple mount (five tubes)

Captain Evans wrapped a handkerchief around his bloody hand. Lieutenant Hagen called his guns, wondering if they would all answer. Gun number four didn't respond.

On the fantail, the rear of the ship, sailors opened a hatch and climbed down a ladder into the steering room. Seaman first class Dusty Rhodes grabbed a three-foot steel arm off the wall and fit the socket end over a shaft leading to the rudder. By turning the steel arm, Dusty and another sailor turned the rudder. With the electric motor down, they would have to steer the ship with muscle power.

Shell splashes spouted like geysers beside the ship. Smoke and steam poured up from the engine room through three gaping holes in the deck. Sailors crawled up ladders and stretched out their arms for help. Men on deck pulled their wounded shipmates out of the inferno and carried them to sickbay.

Hagen wanted to get the guns firing again, and so he called out the target. Soon, flashes burst from the 5-inch guns, followed by an echo of booms. For a moment the ship rolled sideways under the force of the blasts. In truth, the battle was just beginning.

CHAPTER 2

The War Begins

WAR BEGAN IN EUROPE IN 1939 WHEN Germany invaded Poland. Britain and France had promised to protect Poland, and so they declared war on Germany. By late 1941 Germany had defeated France and was fighting a desperate battle against Britain across the waters of the Atlantic Ocean, on the sands of North Africa, and in the skies over Europe. Germany's ally, Japan, decided it was time to act. On December 7, 1941 Japanese aircraft attacked Pearl Harbor in Hawaii. All-out war spread to Asia and the Pacific. But the two proud nations, America and Japan, had started on this dangerous path ten years earlier.

During the 1930s war clouds grew over Asia. In 1931 Japan invaded Manchuria, the northeast province of China. In 1937 the Japanese army invaded the rest of China. The United States government grew angry, demanding that Japan withdraw its troops. Japan refused and secretly made plans to invade other territories in Asia.

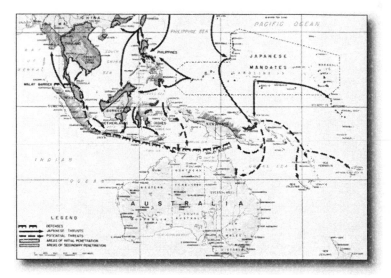

Japanese advances in the Southwest Pacific and Southeast Asia areas during the first five months of the Pacific Campaign of World War II

The Philippines, the Dutch East Indies and Singapore were high on the list.

In 1941 Japan imported most of its oil and scrap iron from the United States. Japan was making warships out of American iron and powering them with American oil. The United States decided to cut off the supply until Japan retreated from China. The Japanese military leaders did not want to retreat. Instead, they set the next part of their plan in motion. On November 27, 1941 almost the entire Japanese fleet sailed east toward Hawaii. For the next ten days they kept radio silence, communicating with signal flags and blinkered lights.

USS *Arizona* at Pearl Harbor

On December 7, 1941 the Japanese fleet was in position 200 miles northwest of Hawaii. Six Japanese carriers launched 183 planes toward Pearl Harbor, where the U.S. battle fleet sat at anchor. They soared over the ocean, arriving at 7:55 a.m. It was Sunday, so most of the U.S. sailors were still asleep.

Seven battleships of the Pacific Fleet were anchored next to Ford Island. One more battleship, the USS *Pennsylvania*, was in dry dock. Japanese warplanes swooped in, peppering the eight warships with bombs and torpedoes.

Caught by surprise, the Americans could only watch the first bombs plummet toward the steel decks. Sailors rushed to their anti-aircraft guns, and a few fighter planes took off from Wheeler Field, but they couldn't stop the onslaught. At 8:54 a second wave of 163 Japanese warplanes soared over the smoldering U.S. fleet. Japanese fighters buzzed nearby airfields while more bombs whistled toward the anchored ships.

When it was over, four battleships settled to the bottom of the harbor, and the other four were badly damaged. Japan had begun its conquest of the Pacific.

CHAPTER 3

The Captain

ERNEST EVANS JOINED THE NAVY IN 1926 AS an ordinary sailor, but within a year his commander recognized his talent and recommended him for the "fleet exams." Evans passed the tests. He entered the U.S. Naval Academy, the college that trained the Navy's officers.

After graduating, Evans served on several ships including a battleship, a cruiser, and two destroyers. Battleships had over a foot of armor and cruisers had several inches of steel plate to protect them. Destroyer hulls were only 3/4 of an inch thick. Their deck armor was even thinner, just 5/8 of an inch. Sailors called them "tin cans."

Destroyer skins were so thin that sailors with bunks next to the hull could hear ocean waves lapping against the metal shell as they fell asleep. This thin armor made destroyers vulnerable to enemy fire but also made them light and fast, while their guns and torpedoes provided a powerful punch.

Cadet Ernest Evans, at the U.S. Naval Academy, Annapolis, Maryland

Evans was Cherokee. If he had been born a few hundred years earlier, he might have ridden into battle in the mountains of Tennessee on a spotted horse, carrying a lance that dangled eagle feathers. But Evans was born in 1908, so instead of a horse, this warrior would have a ship. Instead of sprinting across the mountains, he'd coast over the Pacific Ocean. Instead of a lance, he'd have five-inch guns, torpedoes and depth charges. When war came to the Pacific in 1941, Evans was on a front line destroyer, which was exactly where he wanted to be.

Lieutenant Commander Ernest Evans was at sea aboard the old four-stack destroyer USS *Alden* when he heard the news that the United States and Japan were at war. After the Japanese Navy bombed the U.S. fleet at Pearl Harbor, the conflict quickly spread across Asia and the Pacific.

On December 10 the Japanese army invaded the Philippines. While Japanese soldiers swept through the Philippines, Japanese warships moved south to capture the oil fields of the Dutch East Indies.

Evan's ship the *Alden* was one of the Allied ships standing in their way. The Allies were all of the countries fighting Japan—the United States, Britain, Holland (the Dutch) and Australia. In February 1942 five cruisers and nine destroyers from the Allied navies gathered north of Australia, ready for battle.

They sailed into the Java Sea, where they collided with four Japanese cruisers and fourteen Japanese destroyers. Five new destroyers led the allied column, followed by the larger cruisers. Four old destroyers, the *Alden* among them, took up the rear. The older destroyers had to gun their engines and strain every bolt till it rattled to keep up with the newer warships.

The two forces met in the late afternoon of February 27, 1942. Aboard the *Alden,* Evans watched salvos fall beside the lead ship. Japanese rounds soon found their mark. Shells ripped through the British cruiser *Exeter* and the British destroyer *Electra*. A torpedo struck a Dutch destroyer, splitting it in two. The bow and stern jackknifed up into the air, and both sections sank quickly. As the *Alden* laid smoke to cover the wounded ships, an order came for the destroyers to make a torpedo attack.

An officer aboard the *Alden* said, "I knew the old four-stackers would have to save the day." Everyone in the pilothouse laughed, and the *Alden* swung in to fire its torpedoes. New destroyers were not only fast but also had torpedo mounts that could rotate side to side. The *Alden* and the other old tin cans had fixed mounts. Each ship fired six starboard torpedoes and then did a 180-degree turn to fire its six port side torpedoes.

Of the twelve torpedoes launched by the *Alden*, eight were set to run at a depth of eight feet. These torpedoes

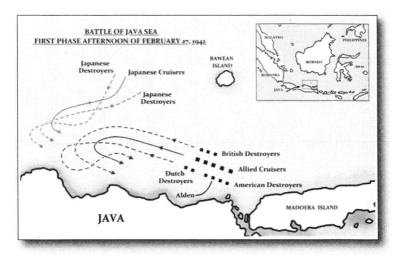

Map of action at Battle of Java Sea

disappeared beneath the waves. The other four, which were set to a depth of four feet, jumped like porpoises through the choppy waters.

The *Alden* had fired from 22,000 yards away, and they scored no hits. The fish, as torpedoes were called, probably ran out of fuel before they reached the retreating enemy. However, the attack gave the damaged British cruiser *Exeter* time to fall back.

The battle broke up into a series of smaller actions that night and the next day. All of these battles turned out badly for the allied fleet. Two Dutch cruisers, a British cruiser, an Australian cruiser and the American cruiser USS *Houston* all went down.

While superior Japanese fleets cornered the Allied cruisers, the *Alden's* destroyer squadron escaped to the south through the Bali Strait, a passage too shallow for the heavier cruisers to follow. On the way they ran into another group of Japanese destroyers. At first the American ships tried to hide, hugging the coastline in the darkness. When they had to sail around a coral reef, the Japanese spotted them and let fly several salvos.

The *Alden* returned fire, but the shells of both sides fell short. Out of torpedoes and outgunned by the newer Japanese ships, the U.S. destroyers laid smoke and held their fire, escaping into the darkness. Though the Allied fleet had been mauled, Evans did not like running away. If I ever have a fighting ship of my own, he told himself, I will never retreat.

The Japanese now had a path open to the oil fields of Dutch Indonesia. They quickly took control of the Dutch colony. With the heavy ships of the Allied fleet on the bottom of the ocean and the Japanese advancing everywhere, the *Alden* retreated south to Australia.

The American destroyers arrived at Fremantle on the western coast of Australia on March 4, 1942. After reaching Fremantle, Captain Coley fell ill, and Evans took command of the *Alden*. The Navy ordered him to sail to Pearl Harbor for convoy duty.

The terror of battle was replaced by the boredom of long days under the Pacific sun as they cruised to Hawaii. The *Alden* spent the next eight months escorting supply ships from California to Hawaii.

TIN CAN SAILORS SAVE THE DAY!

Evans did his job, all the while waiting for a better assignment. Finally, it came. The Navy sent Evans to Seattle, Washington. A new destroyer was coming off the production line, and it needed a captain. Evans would have his fighting ship.

CHAPTER 4

The Gunnery Officer

AS AN OFFICER AT GREAT LAKES NAVAL TRAINING STATION on Lake Michigan, Bob Hagen's job was to assign new recruits to ships. One day five tall, young men walked into the office. They were the Sullivan brothers, and they all wanted to be on the same ship. In fact, the Navy had promised them they would serve together.

Five brothers on one ship sounded like an awful idea to Hagen. What if the ship went down? Hagen sent the young men away. A few days later the commanding officer came up to Hagen with smoke coming out of his ears. The Navy had promised the Sullivan's they would serve together. Who was Hagen to say no? Hagen said he didn't think putting five family members on one ship made sense. The reply from his boss was sharp: "You are twenty-two years old and you don't have to think."

Photo of a young Bob Hagen

Soon the Sullivan brothers boarded their new home, the light cruiser USS *Juneau.* When Hagen's time behind a desk was over, he joined a warship as well. He became the radar officer on the *Aaron Ward,* a destroyer of the U.S. Pacific Fleet.

A few months later the *Aaron Ward* joined an American fleet gathering near Guadalcanal. The *Juneau,* with the five Sullivan brothers aboard, was already there.

Cruisers aren't really big enough to fight battleships, but that's what happened. The Japanese battleships *Hiei* and *Kirishima* sailed southeast toward Guadalcanal with an escort of one cruiser and eleven destroyers. They were coming to bombard Henderson Airfield, a Marine airstrip that had been attacking Japanese troop transports. They were going to silence those pesky planes once and for all.

The United States had only two battleships in its entire Pacific fleet. The admiral in command didn't want to risk his battleships in the narrow waters around Guadalcanal. Instead, he sent two heavy cruisers, three light cruisers and eight destroyers to challenge the Japanese force. The two fleets collided in the middle of a moonless night.

Just before 2 a.m. on November 12, 1942 the fleets headed straight for each other. Straining to tell friend from foe in the darkness, they scraped past each other. The lead American destroyer had to turn hard left to avoid crashing into an enemy vessel. A strange, tense silence followed as American and Japanese ships passed each other but didn't fire.

When the light cruiser *Helena* was lit up by a Japanese searchlight, the gunnery officer rushed to his captain and said, "Permission to open fire, Captain?"

The captain shouted back, "Open fire!"

American and Japanese ships pummeled each other at point blank range. The heavy cruiser *San Francisco* drew up beside the battleship *Hiei* and leveled its guns at the larger warship, blasting the Japanese vessel at the waterline. As water poured into the battleship's engine room, the *Hiei* returned fire, killing the admiral, the captain and the first officer on the bridge of the *San Francisco*. Suddenly, the second officer was in charge.

While the *Hiei* battered the *San Francisco*, it nearly ran over a U.S. destroyer, passing so close that a 20mm gunner aboard the destroyer fired through the portholes on the *Hiei*.

The *Aaron Ward* had been near the back of the battle line. When it caught up, Lieutenant Hagen saw ships aflame everywhere. Hagen used his radar screens to scout a path through the dark waters. A Japanese destroyer turned on its searchlights to locate the American ships. The *Aaron Ward* aimed its guns at the bright lights, blasting the enemy ship until it stopped dead in the water.

Then the *Aaron Ward* felt the sting of enemy fire. A 1,500 pound battleship shell smashed into the ship. Since they were on their way to bombard Henderson Airfield, the Japanese guns were loaded with high-explosive rounds, not armor-piercing rounds. An armor-piercing battleship round might have passed straight through the destroyer's thin armor and out the other side without detonating. High-explosive rounds detonated on impact.

One such shell shattered the deck of the *Aaron Ward*, sending flying bits of metal everywhere. A four-inch bolt ripped into Hagen's thigh. Shards of metal and glass shredded his arm.

Two pharmacist mates rushed over. Hagen tried to wave them off, but they knew better. After giving Hagen two morphine shots, the men put a tourniquet on his arm. Dazed by the morphine, Hagen slid to the ground and fell asleep in a pool of his own blood.

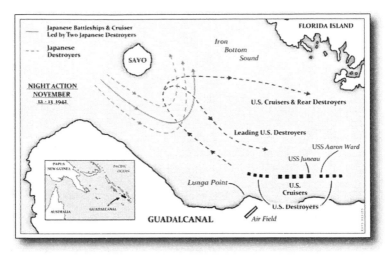

Map of action at Battle of Guadalcanal

Shells from Japanese ships continued to pound the *Aaron Ward*. Water flooded the engine room to a depth of three feet, shutting down the motors and leaving the *Aaron Ward* to drift with the waves. After twenty minutes of pumping and repair work, the gears slowly came back to life. The *Aaron Ward* crawled away from the other burning ships. When Hagen awoke in sickbay, his ship was limping southeast with the other survivors of the battle.

During the night marines at a forward base had been close enough to see the gun flashes and burning ships. They stood on the beach cheering as the U.S. Navy fought off the larger Japanese fleet. The Japanese didn't reach Henderson Airfield.

With dawn came new dangers for both fleets. American dive bombers chased the retreating Japanese ships and sank the crippled *Hiei*. Meanwhile, a Japanese submarine stalked the U.S. warships, slowly creeping into position to fire three torpedoes. One of the torpedoes sank the *Juneau*. None of the Sullivan brothers survived.

The brutal struggle wasn't over. The following night American and Japanese battleships met off Guadalcanal. The USS *Washington* used its radar-guided guns to sink the *Kirishima*. While the *Washington* pummeled the old Japanese battleship, torpedoes struck three American destroyers. All three sank.

It had been a horrific two nights of combat. Fifteen ships had been added to "Iron-bottom Sound," so named because of the number of ships scattered across the seafloor. In the end, the Japanese had been turned back. The airfield on Guadalcanal was safe for now. The U.S. victory at Guadalcanal slowed the Japanese tide. The Japanese still held the oil fields of the Dutch Indies, but their drive south toward Australia had been stopped.

As he healed from his wounds, Bob Hagen got a message. He was to return to America for advanced training. The radar-guided gun system the *Washington* had used to sink the *Kirishima* was being added to the new class of destroyers. Hagen would be the gunnery officer on one of these ships.

CHAPTER 5

The Sailor

ON THE TWO-DAY RIDE FROM KANSAS TO IDAHO, eighteen-year-old Harold "Dusty" Rhodes stared out the window. The train rocked past crystal blue lakes, tree-lined ridges and towering mountains—the first mountains Dusty had ever seen. He thought about his three sisters and mother back home on the farm. He would miss them. He would also miss Tony, the horse he'd ridden to school.

Then his mind drifted to Carol. He remembered driving around town crammed into the back seat of his friend's '37 Ford. When they stopped to pick up some girls, there weren't any seats left, so Carol climbed in and sat on Dusty's lap. Her pretty, red hair fell in his face. Dusty thought *Wow, this is a dream*!

The long train ride ended at Farragut Naval Training Station, a boot camp in Idaho where the Navy turned farm hands and city boys into sailors. When Dusty got off the train, he heard someone inside camp yell, "You're not going to like it here!"

Harold "Dusty" Rhodes home on leave from boot camp, 1943

Dusty wondered exactly what he meant but didn't have time to worry about it. A chief petty officer yelled at the recruits to take off all of their clothes, pack them up in a box and send them home. They couldn't keep them here. They could only wear what the Navy gave them. Then a bunch of naked recruits walked into the next room where the quartermaster threw uniforms at them.

Home on leave - July 1945

Dusty in uniform, home on leave, July 1945

Dusty also got his "boots"—white leggings that were worn above the shoes and looked like boots. It was easy to tell the difference between instructors and recruits because recruits wore these white leggings and instructors didn't. The new guys had to wear these "boots" until they graduated, and so they called themselves boots and their school boot camp.

Next the recruits got a tetanus shot and took a physical fitness test. The young men were still sore from the shot when they had to do pull-ups and push-ups while a petty officer yelled at them. Dusty began to understand why someone had yelled, "You're not going to like it here."

That night Dusty and the other boots moved in to the barracks—long halls with rows of bunk beds. There was no place to put anything down, just like a ship. Dusty put all of his clothes in a sea bag and hung it on his bunk. A sea bag was like a big duffel bag. Then he made his bed, covering the worn-out mattress with a cotton sheet and wool blanket. Climbing into bed that night, Dusty wondered what the next day would bring.

At five in the morning a bugle screeched. The recruits hurried outside for exercises, lining up in a field beside the barracks.

They started with some stretching as boots swung their arms down to touch one toe and then the other. A band played "Anchors Away" and other tunes to help the men keep the rhythm. Next the men did jumping jacks, chin ups, and held a wooden rifle over their heads while they leaned side to side. Then it was time for a 300-yard dash, followed by leg squats. The men bent their knees and leapt as high as they could go. Their stomachs were growling with hunger when the breakfast bell rang.

Every day after morning exercises the boots ate a quick but large breakfast of eggs, bacon, potatoes and oatmeal. Then it was off to a classroom, a practice range, the pool, or the lake. Over the next seven weeks they marched, tied knots, learned to fight fires, qualified on the M1 rifle,

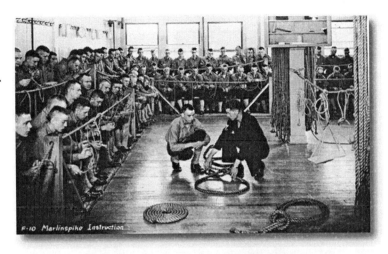

Top: Boots learning to tie knots

Bottom: Men rowing whale boat on lake

practiced reading maps, and rowed whaleboats on the lake. They marched so much that the soles fell off their shoes. Within a few weeks they had to visit the quartermaster to get new ones.

The boots all took a swimming test, which was hard for those who hadn't grown up around water. Dusty dog-paddled around the pool. It was the only stroke he knew. Later they practiced the abandon ship drill by climbing down a cargo net into a pool. The instructor said, "If there are sharks in the water, kick and splash at them. It will scare them away." He made it sound easy.

The men ate dinner and headed back to the barracks. Worn out by a day of endless drill, Dusty climbed into bed and fell asleep to the sound of "Taps" playing over the loudspeaker.

A few hours later a man tapped him. "Rhodes, wake up. It's your turn for guard duty."

Dusty rolled out bed, took the dummy rifle from the other recruit, and stepped outside. He marched back and forth in front of the barracks for two hours in the dead of night. It was a little scary at first being alone in the dark, cold night. After a few weeks he got used to it, and it was just part of the job.

At the end of his shift, he went back inside and tapped the next man. "Thompson, wake up. It's your turn for guard duty."

Time flew by. When graduation day came, Dusty was no longer a boot. He was a sailor. Now it was time to get on another train. This one would take him all the way to Bremerton, Washington where he would meet his captain and board his ship.

CHAPTER 6

The Ship

IN THE TACOMA SHIPYARD SPARKS FLEW. Workers welded together large sheets of metal on the USS *Johnston*, a new destroyer that would soon be home to 330 men. The *Johnston*, like all ships, was born in dry dock when its keel was laid down. Next workers bolted on great spars that crossed the keel at right angles. Then the bulkheads, large walls of steel, came down and divided the ship into eighty-foot sections.

After the bulkheads were in and the sides bolted on, the main deck was laid down. Once that was in place, workers built the deckhouses on top of the main deck. The wardroom, where the officers ate, was on this level. The galley, where the sailors ate, was here as well. The officers had cushioned benches around a long wooden table. The sailors sat on round stools and hard, rectangular benches wrapped around metal tables.

The deckhouse also held sickbay, the laundry room, and the ammunition handling rooms for guns two, three

The USS *Johnston* (DD-557)

and four. The superstructure level, which was above the deckhouses, held the torpedo tubes and the 40mm gun mounts as well as the radio room.

Directly above the radio room was the bridge. All the way forward on the bridge was the pilothouse—that's where the Captain Evans would sit. He had a chair in the right corner of the room. From that seat he'd give orders to the helmsman and the radio operators and lean over to check the compass.

The day the ship was launched, though, it wasn't quite finished. When the *Johnston* slid down a slope greased with ripe bananas, it was just a ship. It wasn't a warship yet. That happened when the vessel was towed dockside and cranes start dropping ammunition on deck.

Launch of the USS *Johnston*, March 25, 1943

USS *Johnston* commissioning ceremony

Meanwhile, electricians and plumbers climbed aboard to get the phones, lights and faucets working.

Another important piece of equipment was brought aboard the *Johnston*: a car-sized box with dials. It was the world's first true computer. Men turned dials to enter the ship's speed and direction, the wind speed, and the enemy's speed, direction and distance. With all of that information, the Mark 1A computer calculated a "fire solution" and aimed the guns automatically at the target chosen by gunnery officer Bob Hagen.

All the while the "stable element," a gyroscope inside a box the size of a refrigerator, corrected for the ship's roll in the ocean. It even worked at night or in clouds because Hagen could use radar to choose targets, just as the *Washington* had done at Guadalcanal.

Once fitted out, the *Johnston's* first crew came aboard, and the ship came to life. It was time for the *Johnston* to be commissioned as DD-557, the 557th destroyer in the history of the U.S. Navy.

On October 27, 1943 the crew lined up at the commissioning ceremony. Captain Evans stood at the podium. His voice boomed out at his crew and the audience.

"This is a fighting ship. I intend to go in harm's way, and anyone who doesn't want to go along had better get off right now." The men standing at attention only had time to take a breath before he went on. "Now that I have a fighting ship, I will never retreat from an enemy force."

Almost exactly one year later the USS *Johnston* and its crew encountered a huge enemy force, and, true to his word, Captain Evans did not retreat.

CHAPTER 7

Life at Sea

THE YEAR IN BETWEEN HAD ITS HIGH POINTS. The ship sailed south to San Diego. On the way the crew tested their new ship and got used to the equipment. Captain Evans revved the engines to maximum, practiced high-speed turns and threw the engines into reverse. Bob Hagen perched himself above the bridge in the gun director and tested the automatic aiming mechanisms on the guns. Dusty learned how to load and fire a 20mm antiaircraft gun.

When they stopped in San Francisco Bay, Captain Evan's son, Ernest, Jr., came aboard. Sailors slept in bunks below deck, and officers shared cabins on the main deck. The captain had two cabins of his own. His larger cabin was on the main deck. His sea cabin, which was a small room with a bed and toilet, was behind the pilothouse on the bridge. That's where Ernest, Jr. stayed.

Ernest, Jr. ran around the ship, had coffee with the petty officers, ate bacon with the officers and watched men fire the guns. He followed his dad around as the crew tested the engines, the rudder and all the other systems. One day they went to flank speed and then did a full stop. The *Johnston's* own wake crashed over the fantail, but the ship stopped as expected. After a few days, they dropped Ernest, Jr. off at a naval base in San Francisco Bay. Soon the *Johnston* was on its way across the Pacific.

The *Johnston* traveled to Hawaii and then arced south toward the Solomon Islands. On the way, the ship stopped to shell Japanese positions in the Marshall Islands. Hagen directed the guns as the *Johnston* pounded Japanese fortifications. The job of the Navy ships was to "soften up" the Japanese defenses before Marines and soldiers stormed ashore. After American forces captured the islands, the *Johnston* continued south toward the Solomon Islands

When it reached the equator, it was time for the "Crossing the Line" ceremony. All of the sailors who had never crossed the equator had to go through an initiation ceremony. One sailor dressed up as Neptune, god of the sea. Another was Neptune's wife. Since there were no women aboard, one sailor put on a dress and a bra. Of course, they needed a baby. The crew usually chose the biggest, fattest sailor to be the baby. He put on a diaper and waddled around the ship. It was all great fun—for the men who had crossed the line before and didn't have to go through it.

Hagen had crossed the equator twice, and Evans had crossed it so many times he'd lost track, so they just watched. For all those new to sailing the ocean sea, including officers, it was a hard day. Some ships built a

King Neptune's court for the Crossing the Line ceremony. This photo comes from the *Johnston's* sister ship the USS *Hoel,* but something similar happened on the *Johnston.*

pool on deck out of rubber rafts. Then Neptune threw the new sailors, or "pollywogs," into the pool one at a time. After that, the old sailors, or "shellbacks," would line up with paddles, and the pollywogs would have to run the gauntlet. This was the only time an old sailor might whack a young officer with a paddle.

While Evans and Hagen sauntered on the bridge, Dusty took his licks. He didn't mind so much. It was the last step in joining the crew. When the ceremony was over, he was no longer a pollywog. He was a shellback—a *real* sailor.

After crossing the equator, the *Johnston* took up submarine patrol duty in the Solomon Islands. On May 15, 1944, the ship's sonar picked up an underwater object. They checked to make sure there were no American submarines in the area. When they got the news that there weren't, Captain Evans knew they had an enemy sub prowling beneath them. He ordered a depth charge attack.

Big barrels filled with explosives were dropped off the stern and launched off the side of the ship. The *Johnston* crisscrossed the area and listened for the submarine's motor. The sonar operator heard a series of small explosions—the depth charges—and then one big blast. When pieces of the submarine and bits of oil floated to the surface, they knew the hunt had been successful.

In July the *Johnston* teamed up with the USS *Pennsylvania*, an old battleship that had been damaged at Pearl Harbor. Resting in dry dock during the attack, the *Pennsylvania* had avoided torpedo strikes. Workers repaired the ship, and it sailed west to join the fight. Together the new destroyer and the old battleship bombarded Japanese positions on the island of Guam.

Later, wounded Marines were brought aboard the *Johnston* because it had a doctor. Seeing those young men bleeding and dying, Dusty felt a deep sense of pity but didn't think it would happen to him.

Dusty sat long hours in the radar room, watching the green cursor flash around the circular screen. His mind drifted to his family and Carol. He could still smell her red hair.

Other jobs filled his days as well. Waves splashed seawater onto the deck and machinery. The saltwater rusted the steel ship, and so the men were constantly chipping off old paint and putting on new paint. Scraping off the red rust and flaky paint, Dusty missed his family back in Kansas. As the day wore on and he joked with the other sailors, he realized that the ship was becoming his second home and his shipmates were becoming his second family.

About this time Seaman Second Class Dusty Rhodes became Seaman First Class Dusty Rhodes. He also became the cook for petty officers. The man leaving the job told him, "This is the job you want. You only have to serve twelve men in the petty officers' quarters instead of 300 in the mess hall." When Dusty realized that he could eat extra sandwiches and ice cream in the petty officers' quarters, it was an easy decision. He took the job. In fact, he didn't even have to cook. He just carried warm food down from the galley.

Meanwhile, Captain Evans seemed to enjoy setting off the General Quarters siren. This was the alarm that told men to go to their battle stations. He did it so often that the men started calling the *Johnston* "GQ Johnny," short for General Quarters Johnny. Evans knew what he was doing, though. He wanted the men to be ready for battle.

So did Bob Hagen. He drilled them endlessly on loading the guns. They had contests to see how many shells each gun crew could fire in five minutes. Gun number four won. Their prize was a pack of cigarettes for each man. The sailors also learned two back-up ways to fire a shell in the barrel if the powder didn't ignite. The last way was hitting the firing pin with a mallet. No one really wanted to do that, but a mallet sat on the floor of the turret just in case.

Everyone learned to respect Captain Evans, both for his fighting spirit and his knowledge. Once when it was

The USS *Johnston* refueling while underway, alongside an unidentified oiler during the Palau campaign as seen from the USS *Sargent Bay*, September 1944

time to refuel at sea, the other destroyers in the fleet blew their ballast water to make room for the fuel. Evans saw a storm coming and kept the seawater in the ballast tanks.

The whole crew would count their blessings that they had an experienced captain. The storm arrived before the tanker did. The other ships, which were now top heavy, rolled violently in the high waves. With the weight of ballast water holding its centerline, the *Johnston* swayed only a little. They rode out the storm, but their greatest adventure was yet to come.

CHAPTER 8

The Gathering Storm

OCTOBER 23-24, 1944 MARKED THE BEGINNING of the largest naval battle in history. While American troops landed on the island of Leyte in the central Philippines, U.S. submarines torpedoed three Japanese cruisers. The next day, October 24, U.S. carrier pilots sank the super battleship *Musashi*. That night the U.S. Seventh Fleet destroyed two old Japanese battleships.

The Japanese Imperial Navy had sent almost every warship left in its fleet to stop the U.S. invasion of the Philippines. Japan needed food and oil from Southeast Asia. Losing the Philippines would cut off that lifeline. The Japanese attack had failed so far, but more Japanese warships were on the way.

Far to the north four Japanese carriers sailed toward Leyte, but the flight decks were almost empty. Three years of war and taken their toll, and they simply didn't have

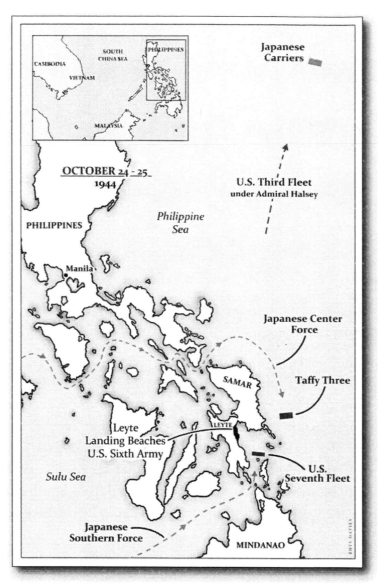

Map of Philippines with arrow showing direction of Japanese Battle Fleet and position of *Johnston's* flotilla, Taffy Three

enough planes and pilots to fill the ships. The carriers were just a decoy. Their job was to lure Admiral Halsey's fleet away so that the battleships of the Japanese Center Force could sneak through the San Bernadino Strait and destroy the American troop ships at Leyte Gulf.

Admiral Halsey commanded the U.S. Third Fleet, the most powerful fleet in the world. Its six battleships, eleven aircraft carriers and host of cruisers and destroyers stretched from horizon to horizon. Halsey's job was to guard the northern approach to Leyte Gulf.

When the Japanese carriers were spotted to the north, Halsey's own officers warned him that it was a trick. He should leave a squadron of battleships to guard the San Bernadino Strait, they told him. Halsey ignored their advice. He was an aggressive commander, and this was his chance to destroy the Japanese carriers.

Believing that the Japanese battleships of Center Force had retreated after losing the *Musashi*, he sailed north with his entire fleet to chase the empty Japanese carriers. During the night the remaining four battleships of the Japanese Center Force, along with eight cruisers and eleven destroyers, slipped through the San Bernadino Strait.

Directly in their path lay the *Johnston* and a small force of escort carriers, destroyers and destroyer escorts. The escort carriers' planes attacked Japanese fortifications on Leyte, while the destroyers and destroyer escorts protected the carriers from submarines. The official name of this group of ships was Task Unit 77.4.3, but everyone called them Taffy Three. As the giant ships of Japanese Center Force bore down on Taffy Three and the invasion fleet, the *Johnston* quietly cruised back and forth listening for submarines.

For the moment none of the men aboard the *Johnston* knew what the day would require of them. Then a scout plane spotted approaching ships. Captain Evans called Admiral Sprague, who was in charge of Taffy Three, to ask about the contact. Admiral Sprague said not to worry. They were Halsey's ships. Still a little anxious about the contact, the men went back to their morning routines.

Captain Evans returned to his sea cabin. Up on the gun director's platform, Lieutenant Hagen asked a mess boy to bring him a fried-egg sandwich and some coffee. Dusty's morning routine was bringing hot food down the ladder from the kitchen to the chiefs' quarters. Today he was carrying bacon and hot biscuits.

The clock in the pilothouse showed 6:50 a.m. That's when a sailor on the torpedo mount saw splashes beside the ship. At first he thought it was dolphins playing.

CHAPTER 9

First Contact

ON THE BRIDGE LIEUTENANT WELCH, A TALL, young officer with dark hair and a dark mustache, leaned over the rail to sniff breakfast odors wafting up from the galley. Then, he too saw splashes. Watching the geysers erupt off the stern, Welch looked up, searching the sky for enemy planes. When he realized that radar would have spotted incoming planes, he knew it could only be one thing. Welch ran around to the starboard side, where he saw the pagoda-style masts of Japanese warships poking over the horizon to the northwest.

As officer of the watch, Lieutenant Welch knew it was time to wake the skipper. Captain Evans burst out of his cabin giving orders.

"All hands to general quarters. All engines ahead flank. Left full rudder."

The helmsman turned hard left, the pilot pushed the throttle lever all the way forward, and the general quarters alarm rang, followed by the announcement, "All hands to

Size Comparison of the *Johnston* and Its Opponents off Samar

Destroyer USS *Johnston*   2,800 Tons   Five 5-inch guns

Battleship *Kongo*   36,300 Tons   Eight 14-inch guns

Heavy Cruiser *Kumano*   13,900 Tons   Ten 8-inch guns

Light Cruiser *Yahagi*   7,700 Tons   Six 6-inch guns

Destroyer *Nowaki*   2,500 Tons   Four 5-inch guns

RHYS DAVIES

Chart showing comparative sizes of Japanese and American ships involved in the battle off Samar, October 25, 1944

battle stations. This is no drill. We are about to engage a major portion of the Japanese fleet."

With the engines revving up to maximum speed, Dusty Rhodes left the sizzling bacon and warm biscuits on the table and made his way to a 20mm gun on the stern. Dusty's crew couldn't do anything yet because the Japanese were way beyond the range of their small gun. They heard shells whistle overhead and crash into the water behind them. While Rhodes waited for his part in the battle, the bridge came to life.

Captain Evans gave the order to lay a smoke screen. If they were outgunned, at least they would make the escort carriers hard to see.

Engineers threw extra oil into the boilers, and billows of black smoke poured out of the stacks. Sailors also rushed to the fantail, where they switched on chemical canisters that made white smoke. Soon the destroyer was putting up a wall of zebra-patterned haze as it charged at Japanese Center Force.

Shells landed all around the *Johnston*, but Captain Evans knew what to do. He chased the splashes, trusting that two shells would never land in exactly the same place. Evans' strategy worked because the Japanese gunners were trained to adjust their aim after ever miss. They were always shooting at the place he had just been.

Fourteen-inch and eight-inch shells plummeted into the water beside and behind the *Johnston*. An eight-inch round landed off the bow and sprayed Hagen with red dye. The Japanese put dye in their shells so they could

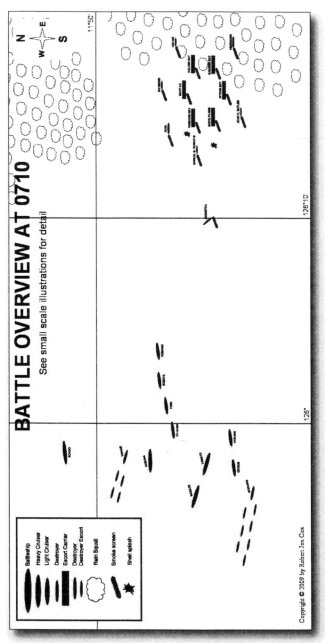

Map of fleets at 0710, showing the *Johnston* making its solitary charge at the Japanese fleet (*Courtesy of Robert Jon Cox & www.bosamar.com*)

Destroyer and destroyer escort laying smoke screen during the battle

track the splashdowns and adjust their aim. Before long a rainbow of purple, red, green and yellow water surrounded the destroyer.

Bob Hagen was waiting to get within 18,000 yards, the maximum range of the ship's five-inch guns. In the meantime the guns were loaded. In each turret a sailor lifted a gunpowder case into the loading tray. Then the loader took a fifty-four-pound round out of the hoist and placed it in front of the powder. Finally, the rammer pushed them both forward into the gun barrel and locked the breech. The guns were ready to fire.

When they'd closed the distance, Hagen looked across the ocean and chose a target. It was the cruiser *Kumano*, the lead ship in the Japanese line. Men beside Hagen in the gun director used telescopes to mark the location and range of the target. With this information the Mark 1A computer automatically aimed all five guns.

Hagen pulled the trigger. The firing pins struck the powder cases, and five shells traced a low arc over the ocean

After the men reloaded, the computer turned the guns and lowered the elevation. With a pull of Hagen's finger, another five rounds blasted the cruiser.

As each gun recoiled, the empty powder case popped out of the barrel. The hot case man, who wore long gloves that went past his elbow, swung his arms down and batted it through a chute behind the gun. A gust of air cleared the barrel of leftover gunpowder, and another shell came up the hoist. After the third salvo, the *Johnston's* crew saw smoke and fire on the *Kumano*. They were scoring hits already.

You can't sink a big ship with a small shell, though, and so Captain Evan's next order was no surprise.

"We can't go down with our fish still aboard. Stand by for torpedo attack."

CHAPTER 10

A Wounded Ship

JACK BECHDEL, THE TORPEDO OFFICER, looked through a telescope to get a bearing on the *Kumano*. He ordered mount one to aim 110 degrees to starboard and mount two to aim 125 degrees to starboard. Sailors cranked both mounts into position.

Evans shouted, "Fire torpedoes!"

Men on the mounts pulled the firing levers at three-second intervals. One after another ten torpedoes blasted out the tubes, flew over the men on the rail and tilted toward the ocean, their propellers spinning in the air. They plunged into the waves, where their prop blades bit into the water. Ten white wakes fanned out toward the enemy cruisers.

Bechdel reported, "Torpedoes running hot, straight and normal."

As they counted the minutes to impact, their target disappeared into the smoke. Then, just when Bechdel had predicted, they heard two underwater explosions. A few moments later the *Kumano* emerged from the haze, its

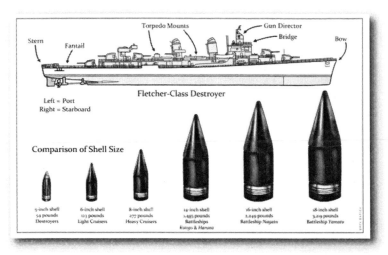

Diagram showing layout of a Fletcher-Class Destroyer and relative shell sizes of both U.S. and Japanese armaments

deck awash in flames. The sailors threw their arms in the air and yelled in celebration. Captain Evans ordered a sharp turn to port. Turning away to the south and then southeast, the *Johnston* hid behind its own smokescreen. They couldn't dodge the enemy fire forever, though.

In the distance three shells roared out of the battleship *Kongo's* main battery. The giant rounds arced over the water and crashed into the stern of the *Johnston*. One hit the engine gears. Another smashed the steam turbine, and the final shell in the salvo demolished the rear boiler, spraying steam and shrapnel all over the

A smoking USS *Gambier Bay* with shell splashes nearby

sailors. The left propeller shaft stopped turning, leaving the *Johnston* at half power.

Dusty Rhodes was manning his 20mm gun when a man came up from below, looked at him, and collapsed on deck. He was the first dead man Dusty saw that day. Steam escaping from the boilers had cooked him.

As men in the engine room crawled out of the inferno, three six-inch rounds streaked toward the *Johnston*. One hit the aft smokestack, while the other two crashed into the bridge.

Several men were killed instantly, and Lieutenant Bechdel lay on the floor groaning. He complained about

Map of fleets at 0750 (*Courtesy of Robert Jon Cox &
www.bosamar.com*)

pain in his arms but didn't seem to realize that one of his
legs was missing below the knee. Captain Evans had two
fingers blown off. Evans, whose shirt was burned off his
back and hanging in tatters, took a handkerchief and
wrapped it around his bloody hand. Dr. Robert Browne
rushed toward Evans. The captain waved him off.

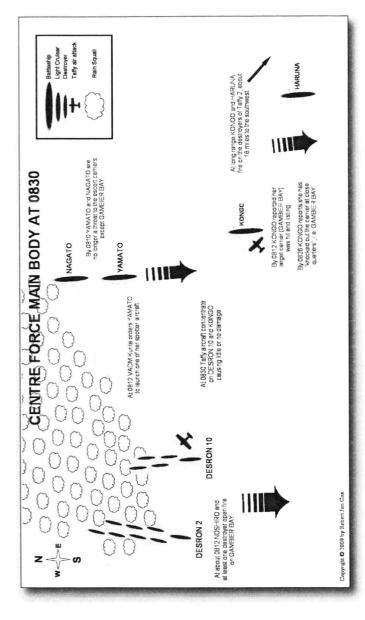

CENTRE FORCE MAIN BODY AT 0830

Battleship
Light Cruiser
Destroyer
Taffy air attack

Rain Squall

By 0810 YAMATO and NAGATO are no longer a threat to the escort carriers, except GAMEIER BAY

At long range KONGO and HARUNA fire on the destroyers of Taffy 2, about 18 miles to the southwest.

NAGATO

YAMATO

HARUNA

KONGO

By 0812 KONGO reported her target carrier (GAMBIER BAY) was hit and listing

By 0826 KONGO reports she has knocked out the carrier at close quarters', i.e. GAMBIER BAY

At 0812 VADM Kurita orders YAMATO to launch one of her spotter aircraft.

At 0830 Taffy aircraft concentrate on DESRON 10 and KONGO causing little or no damage

DESRON 10

DESRON 2

At about 0812 NOSHIRO and at least one destroyer open fire on GAMBIER BAY.

N
E
W
S

Copyright © 2009 by Robert Jon Cox

Map of fleets at 0830 (*Courtesy of Robert Jon Cox & www.bosamar.com*)

"Don't bother me now. Help some of those guys who are hurt."

Sailors rushed to the bridge to remove the dead and wounded. When they arrived, blood was pouring off the bridge like water. The men carried Bechdel to the wardroom where Dr. Browne bandaged his stump. On a normal day, the officers ate their meals in the wardroom. During battle, the ship's doctor did surgery on the dining room table.

Hagen wanted to know how badly the ship was damaged. He yelled, "All stations—control testing!" Then he waited.

"Gun one, aye."

"Gun two, aye."

"Gun three, aye."

"Gun five, aye."

Hagen feared the worst, but soon a message came from gun four. They were alive but had lost power and communication.

Something else had lost power: the rudder. Dusty Rhodes joined a group going below to turn the steering wheel by hand. When Evans called out a course change, the order was phoned to the men in back. Dusty and a fellow sailor turned cranks that pumped hydraulic fluid into the steering wheel. Their arms aching and their brows sweating, they turned the rudder with muscle power.

As sailors cleared the bridge of wounded men, a rain squall kicked up beside the *Johnston*. Evans looked at the dark clouds touching the water. The *Johnston* turned into the clouds, trading the smoke and fire of battle for the rain and wind of a tropical storm. The downpour put out many of the fires raging across the ship.

Gun number four was now on "local control." For the men in gun four this meant taking ranges through a scope and aiming themselves. In the squall they couldn't do anything, but Hagen could.

Guns one and two were undamaged. The fire control computer got a range and direction from the radar, and soon Hagen was firing through the clouds. The men in guns three and five got a target from the computer but had to crank the gun into position themselves because they had lost power. The Japanese, who had nothing like the fire control computer, must have been shocked to see rounds spiraling out of the mist and striking their ships.

So far the *Johnston* had been fighting alone, but that was about to change. A message from Admiral Sprague crackled over the radio.

"Small boys attack. Commence torpedo run."

The "small boys" were the destroyers and destroyer escorts. The *Johnston,* of course, had already charged in and fired its torpedoes. Upon hearing the order, the destroyers *Hoel* and *Heermann* plowed west into the teeth of the Japanese fleet. The destroyer escort *Samuel B. Roberts* followed close behind. Overhead, planes from Taffy Three carriers swooped down on the Japanese fleet, dropping bombs and torpedoes.

When Evans heard the admiral's command over the

radio, he knew he'd spent his torpedoes, but he still had his guns.

"We'll go back in and provide fire support."

With that command the *Johnston* turned back toward the Japanese armada, but it was on half power, out of torpedoes and covered with casualties. Hagen thought to himself *Dear God, I'm in for a swim.*

CHAPTER 11

No Retreat

WHEN THE *JOHNSTON* BROKE THROUGH THE CLOUDS, Dusty Rhodes stood on the deck taking a break from the exhausting work of turning the rudder. He looked to the right to see a remarkable sight. Just a few hundred yards to starboard the *Heermann* barreled out of the clouds. It was plowing straight at the *Johnston*.

"All engines back full!" yelled Captain Evans.

The *Heermann* also threw its engines into reverse. Rhodes watched water churn behind the ship as it tried to back down. With only one engine, the *Johnston* couldn't stop; it could only slow down.

Captain Evans gave the order, "Left full rudder!"

The *Johnston* swung to port, missing the *Heermann* by ten feet. Dusty could almost have reached out and touched the friendly destroyer as it passed by. Dusty and the other men topside cheered, "Hooray!"

The *Heermann* continued on its torpedo run. Meanwhile, Evans told Hagen not to fire at anything unless he could see the ship. They didn't want to shoot the *Hoel, Heermann* or *Roberts*.

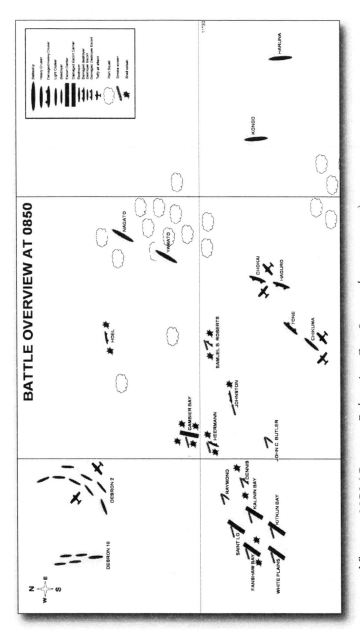

Map of fleets at 0850 (Courtesy Robert Jon Cox & www.bosamar.com)

Breaking through the smoke, a Japanese battleship emerged 7,000 yards to port. *I can sure as hell see that*, thought Hagen.

It was the *Kongo*, which was lobbing fourteen-inch shells over their heads toward the escort carrier *Gambier Bay*. The *Johnston* got off forty-five rounds from its five-inch guns, peppering the *Kongo* with at least fifteen hits. Dusty and two other sailors saw muzzle flashes erupt from the battleship's big guns, so they ran around to the other side and ducked. However, the Japanese warship ignored the *Johnston* and pelted the *Gambier Bay* into a fiery mess.

Back to the southeast Evans saw the Japanese heavy cruisers closing on the escort carriers.

"Attack that cruiser and draw their fire from the escort carriers."

The *Johnston* heeled around and sped toward its fourth gun battle of morning. Back in gun number five, gun captain Clint Carter was spurring his men on to fire faster. Carter was a short, stocky sailor from Texas. He was shooting whatever came up the hoist: armor-piercing shells, high explosive rounds, even star shells—phosphorescent rounds designed to light up an enemy target at night.

The hoist on gun number four was damaged, so men passed shells up the ladder. Dusty stood at the top of the ladder, sweating as he handed the fifty-four-pound shells down the line of men leading to the turret door.

While they battled the enemy cruiser, Evans looked to the west and saw a line of Japanese ships plowing toward the U.S. carriers. The enemy vessels looked like they were getting into position to fire a broadside of torpedoes. Knowing they were the bigger threat, Evans turned to intercept and ordered Hagen to fire on the lead ship.

The lead ship was the light cruiser *Yahagi*, which was followed by four Japanese destroyers. The *Johnston* opened up on the *Yahagi*. The five-inch guns struck the light cruiser twelve times, and it veered off to starboard. Hagen switched his fire to the second ship, scoring several more hits.

In gun number five Clint Carter yelled, "More shells! More shells!"

While the *Johnston's* guns blazed away, an enemy shell hit a 40mm storage locker on the *Johnston*, setting off the ammunition. The explosion sprayed the deck with shrapnel, killing a group of men huddled under the 40mm gun tub. The blast also started fires that spread across the *Johnston*.

Then a most miraculous thing happened. The line of Japanese warships, which could have plowed forward and launched dozens of torpedoes at close range, fired their torpedoes at extreme range instead. Then they turned around and headed north. The Japanese admiral had just ordered a retreat.

With victory so close, it seemed a strange decision. The Japanese battleships had achieved surprise and were close to breaking through to the invasion beachheads, where they could have pounded the American landing fleet and the Army positions ashore.

Years later Admiral Kurita would hint that he didn't want to get trapped between Halsey's battle fleet coming down from the north and the old battleships of the U.S. Seventh Fleet sailing up from the south. Kurita believed he had been given a suicide mission, and he was turning it down. Asked about the decision a few years before his death, Admiral Kurita simply said, "I just couldn't let all of those boys die."

As the Japanese ships sailed away, Evans looked elated. He strutted back and forth on the bridge. "Now I've seen everything!"

On the stern Dusty saw something as well. Three white lines plowed toward the *Johnson*—the unmistakable trail of torpedoes in the water. Both Japanese destroyers and cruisers carried the underwater missiles, and their final salvo was closing in. Dusty's heart pounded as the bubbles crept closer, but the white trails passed just astern.

The *Johnston* sailed safely away from the torpedo wakes, but the battle had its cost. Gun number one was out of action. With flames sprouting up around the bridge, Evans switched his command to the stern, where he leaned over an open hatch and shouted orders to the men cranking the steering wheel.

The *Heermann* rejoined the carrier force and escorted it south, away from the Japanese warships. The *Hoel* and *Gambier Bay* had already slipped beneath the waves while the *Samuel B. Roberts* lay dead in the water, sinking stern first. The *Johnston* was once again alone, and once again it was nearly surrounded.

Four cruisers and four destroyers formed a semicircle around the wounded ship, but the *Johnston's* gunners blazed on. Gun five poured round after round at the enemy ships encircling the *Johnston*. Gun four kept firing as well, but the power was out on the hoist, and the ammunition room was flooding. Men with water up to their shins were passing shells toward the stairway and up to the gun. Meanwhile, Dusty Rhodes took another turn cranking the steering wheel.

A six-inch shell shattered the number two gun. Inside the turret, which only a moment earlier had been full of action, dead men lay limp on the floor. Then an explosion rocked the number one engine, and the *Johnston* ground to a halt. They were dead in the water.

The time had come. Evans looked at his men.

"All hands abandon ship!"

Lieutenant Welch walked forward repeating, "Abandon ship! Abandon ship!"

On his way back down the ship, which was now tilting to port, Welch saw a wounded sailor struggling to get into a life vest. After helping the man into the vest, Welch helped him over the rail and plopped him into the ocean. Now it was Welch's turn. He took off his shoes and dove in.

Evans poked his head into gun turret number four and told the men to abandon ship. Then he turned toward a pile of bodies underneath the 40mm gun mount. "See if any of these men are alive," he ordered. Some sailors checked through the pile, but all of the men were dead.

Dusty Rhodes was turning the steering wheel when

the order came. Someone leaned over the hatch and yelled, "Abandon ship!"

Dusty and his crewmate climbed up the ladder, leaving the steering room empty. The *Johnston* would now drift with the waves. Above deck smoke squeezed into his eyes, and the smell of burnt paint poured into his nose. Soot-covered sailors reached into storage lockers and pulled out life vests as shells continued crashing into the ship.

Dusty made his way to the number four gun, where a floater net rested inside a basket. He tugged and pulled on the twenty foot by twenty foot net laced with cork rings, but it wouldn't budge.

Chuck Campbell, an old friend with a narrow face and close-set eyes, saw him pulling and came over to help. Together they tossed the net into the ocean. Then Dusty jumped in himself. At first he wondered how deep the water was and if he was going to hit the bottom. He didn't need to worry about that. The water below him was 20,000 feet deep.

Coming up from the wardroom with life vests, an officer saw Jack Bechdel trying to get over the side. His stump was bandaged, but he was too weak to climb over the rail. The officer helped Bechdel into the water. Then a shell landed behind the officer, blasting him thirty feet into the air and tossing him into the ocean.

By now sailors on the foredeck didn't have to jump because the main deck was level with the water. As the bow sank, they simply stepped into the ocean and began swimming away.

High above deck in the gun director, Hagen had missed the order to abandon ship. When he looked through the smoke, he couldn't see anybody below except the dead. Realizing what was happening, he turned to his crew. "What the hell are we doing here? Let's abandon ship."

The other five men had been waiting for those words. They were out of the gun director and down the ladder in a flash. Hagen himself stood still for a moment, as if in a dream. When he climbed down he tried to walk to the rear, but piles of twisted metal and lifeless men blocked the way. Hagen turned and walked toward the bow, where he slowly took off his shoes and dove into the water.

Looking back at the *Johnston*, Hagen saw Dr. Browne pulling wounded men out of the wardroom.

Hagen yelled, "Abandon ship!"

Dr. Browne yelled something that Hagen couldn't hear and headed back inside. Seconds later a shell crashed into the wardroom. Watching the explosion shatter the infirmary and kill his friend, Hagen cried. For half a minute, he let it all pour out. Then he got a hold of himself and realized he had to put some distance between himself and the sinking ship if he wanted to avoid being sucked down. Hagen began swimming away.

Another shell hit the *Johnston*, blasting the men on the port side with a blinding yellow flash. Bob Sochor, a fair-haired sailor with a long face and long fingers, woke up with stinging pain in his back and dead bodies all around him. He realized that almost everyone had already abandoned ship. Sochor made his way to the stern, and as he did he saw Captain Evans going forward. They stared blankly at each other without saying a word. That was the last time anyone remembers seeing Evans.

When he got to the fantail, Sochor couldn't find a life vest, so he just jumped in. He swam toward a group gathering 100 yards off the stern. Exhausted halfway there, he met another survivor and grabbed on to him.

"I can't swim and this life vest can't hold both of us up," the man said.

"Don't worry. I just want to rest for a moment."

Looking back at their ship, which was dipping below the waves, Sochor went on, "Take your last look at the *Johnston*."

Dusty was taking his last look as well. For him it was like watching his house burn down. The *Johnston* had been his home for the last year. Now, black with soot and still smoking, it slipped below the waves.

As the men swam away from their ship, a Japanese destroyer approached and poured rounds into the burning hulk. Then the enemy ship's guns fell silent, and the men of the *Johnston* could hear strange sounds. Japanese sailors lined up along the rail, talking and laughing. Some pointed at the Americans and flashed the "number 1" sign.

When the *Johnston* was afloat and the guns were working, the men could fight back. Now they were helpless, and for some of them this was the first time they were truly afraid. They rose and fell with the cresting waves, expecting the Japanese to drop depth charges into the water. It looked like the Japanese were lowering their anti-aircraft guns to fire on the survivors.

The Japanese had been known to shoot men instead of rescuing them, so the sailors braced themselves for the worst. A few got ready to dive under the water.

That's when a Japanese officer turned to face the anti-aircraft guns and held up his hands. The Japanese sailors let go of the gun cranks and just looked at the ragged sailors floating in the water.

In the end, the Japanese didn't drop explosives, and they didn't shoot the Americans. Instead, an officer on the bridge stood very straight, raised his hand to his hat, and saluted. Before sailing away, a man on the stern threw something at the Americans floating in the water.

Someone yelled, "It's a grenade!"

But when it plopped into the water beside Clint Carter, it didn't explode. He swam over and fished it out of the waves.

"No, it's not. It's a can of tomatoes."

Carter read the label, which told him it had been packed in Arkansas three years earlier, before the war had started.

CHAPTER 12

Adrift at Sea

THE SUN BEAT DOWN ON THE SURVIVORS as they watched the Japanese fleet retreat to the north. A large group, including Dusty and Hagen, gathered around two rafts and two floater nets that they tied together with rope.

After the enemy ships left, Dusty just wanted to keep his head above the water. He and the other men wrapped their arms through the floater net and held on as they rose and fell with each wave.

They hoped a friendly plane would spot them. Soon a U.S. Navy torpedo bomber flew by and dipped its wings, which meant they'd been spotted. There was nothing to do now but hang on and wait for rescue.

A little while later they saw a dark triangle poke above the surface. It had a splash of white on the tip.

"What was that?" someone asked.

The men couldn't see very well in the rising swells, but then a long gray body with white splotches on its tail swam right next to them. Dusty's heart skipped a beat.

A WWII life raft, much like the one the men clung to during their ordeal

"Shark!"

The man next to Dusty grabbed his life vest and pulled him close. They squeezed themselves together and faced out. Like a group of bison under attack from wolves, they tried to make a tight circle. Another dorsal fin popped up and faded away. Then one came close. It swayed side to side, bent toward the men, and reached in with its nose.

"Get away!" They yelled, kicking at it and splashing the water, just as they'd been taught back in boot camp.

The sharks swam slowly, circling several times before coming in to bump the men. Then, as quickly as they had come, the sharks melted away.

Oceanic white tip sharks like this attacked the men repeatedly

After a few heart-pounding moments, the man next to Dusty said, "I think they're gone."

They were gone, but they'd be back.

Still, everyone expected to be rescued by nightfall. Surely by now the plane had reported their position and ships were on the way. What the sailors didn't know was that the pilot had reported the wrong position. The rescue ships would soon be searching for them, but twenty miles too far to the north. To make matters worse, the ocean current was carrying the men to the southwest, away from the search area.

Like everyone else, Lieutenant Hagen expected to be plucked from the water any time. He felt confident enough to hand out the small rations stored in a supply canister. Each man got two swallows of water, a cube of spam and part of a biscuit. There should have been more fresh water, but the barrels hadn't been changed in over a year, and some of the water had spoiled.

Hagen also lit a few cigarettes to pass around. Each man took two or three drags before handing the cigarette on to the next guy. Soon the cigarettes were soaked, but men tried to inhale anyway. One sailor pulled apart a wet cigarette and slipped the leaves inside his cheek like chewing tobacco.

Afternoon drifted into evening, and the sun fell toward the horizon. The sailors kept looking across the ocean, hoping to see a friendly ship. None came. Soaked and sunburned, the sailors started to feel dryness in their throats. The battle had started right before breakfast, so most of them hadn't eaten since the night before. Everyone was hungry, thirsty and tired.

For the men with burns, being in the ocean was unbearable. The saltwater tortured them, scratching and gnawing at the raw skin. For others it was the slow drip of blood into the ocean that sapped their energy.

It was already too late for some of the men. They were dying. Pharmacist mate Clayton Schmuff gave them morphine to ease the pain. Before jumping overboard, he had grabbed a case of medicine. His morphine shots helped men die a little softer death.

Ed Haubrich had a severe leg wound. When Dusty accidentally touched it underwater, he screamed. A little while later, Ed looked at Dusty again.

A U.S. Navy fighter plane, similar to this Grumman TBF Avenger, spotted the survivors but the pilot reported the wrong position

"Hey, Dusty, would you give me a sandwich?"

Dusty had sometimes brought Ed food while he was on watch, so Dusty decided a gentle lie was the best response.

"Sure, I'll get you one in a minute."

Ed didn't say anything else. When the life had gone out of him, Schmuff took his dog tags and Dusty took off his life vest. Then they let him drift away. This simple sort of last rites happened several more times during the night.

They gave the vest to a man who didn't have one.

A little later they heard a motor in the distance.

Everyone perked his head up and swiveled around, trying to get a bearing on the sound. A shape loomed out of the darkness. Rescue! Men started waving their hands and yelling, but when it drew closer they recognized the pagoda-style bridge of a Japanese ship.

Someone whispered, "Quiet! Everyone quiet!"

The ocean went silent except for the lapping of the waves and the drone of the motor. With searchlights crisscrossing the ocean, the sound receded into the distance. It was a Japanese ship, a destroyer that had been sent back to pick up survivors of a Japanese cruiser sunk during the battle.

No one wanted to be a prisoner-of-war. The men had heard the horrible tales of what had happened to U.S. soldiers in Japanese prison camps—men starving to death and being beaten to death. They'd take their chances with the deep, dark ocean. They still expected rescue at any moment.

CHAPTER 13

The Sharks Return

A BRIGHT MOON LIT UP THE OCEAN. Bob Sochor wondered if sharks could see at night, but the sharks didn't need to see. Men with wounds ranging from small cuts to huge gashes seeped blood into the ocean. The sharks smelled the blood, and it marked the way to the men.

First one fin sliced through the moonlit waves, and then more came. Surfacing into the humid tropical air, their bodies broke up the phosphorescent plankton on the ocean. An eerie glow showed their path through the water. It led to the sailors. The sharks circled, then dipped below the waves.

The men held their breath, but they couldn't see a thing in the dark waters. Not knowing when the sharks would strike was the worst part. One bumped a sailor's leg. The man closed his fist and hit the shark on the nose. It swam away, slowly. More fins popped up, brushed side to side and sunk below the surface.

In the dark depths a mouth full of teeth accelerated to attack speed, pushing the water out of the way and clamping down on Clint Carter's back.

"Ouch!" was Carter's curdled yell.

The shark pulled him under. Carter reached for the surface, grabbing on to Chuck Campbell's shoulders and pulling him down. The shark released its grip and bit again. The sharp teeth pinched and tore him, but then the pain faded. The shark let go, swimming away with a big chunk of his life vest but only a small chunk of his flesh. Blood dripped out the wound, and the other men pushed Carter into the raft.

The long, gray shapes had dark eyes the size of a dime. They weren't angry, just hungry. They looked at Dusty. He prayed, "God, let me live through this, and I promise I'll live a good life."

Dusty and the other men kicked and splashed, but the sharks kept coming. One bit a gunner's mate on the upper leg, crushing his bone. He screamed, and the life drained out of him. When he died, his friends slipped off his vest and let him drift away. Thrashing fins and swinging tails surrounded the corpse. One man couldn't help but add, "Well, I guess we're feeding the sharks."

Chuck Campbell, the man who had helped Dusty throw the floater net into the water, got a piercing bite on his calf muscle, but the shark let go.

Campbell gasped, "I guess I'm too salty for him. That's what happens when you're in the Navy this long."

As the night wore on and the sharks swam off, the

sailors began taking roll call to keep awake. They counted off by numbers, going round the net over and over.

Other dangers lurked. Thirst drove some of the men mad. Clint Carter told everyone he was going down below to get fresh water out of the *Johnston's* drinking fountains. Then he stood up on the perimeter tube and dove into the center of the raft. He landed on a few sleeping friends.

Carter regained his senses, but not all of the men did.

Floating beside the net, Dusty and a shipmate talked to pass the time. But the man had lost too much blood and drunk too much seawater.

"Let's go to the corner and get a cocktail."

"No, not now," Dusty answered.

"C'mon. Let's go." The man grabbed him.

"No, stay here."

The man swam off, and no one saw him again.

Other men didn't swim away. They fell asleep and drifted away. Clarence Trader was slipping in and out of consciousness when he heard a voice.

"Trader, wake up! God damn it. Get back to the net."

Clarence realized that he'd floated off. He swam back to the floater net with his shipmate, though in the darkness he couldn't see who it was. When they reached the group, the other men tied Clarence to the net so that he wouldn't drift off again. Now he felt better. If he was going to die, he wanted to die here, among friends. Then it wouldn't be so bad.

A few hours later the sun came up, and the men felt sure they'd see friendly ships on the horizon. But morning brought only a scorching sun and parched throats. Chuck Campbell and five other men decided to swim for shore.

Campbell's long arms grabbed a plank and kicked against the water with the mountains of Samar in the distance. Fifty miles separated the survivors from the Philippine island, but some of the peaks were tall enough to be seen on a clear day. The scorching sun burned off layers of skin, leaving the men with scars. They kept swimming.

After struggling for hours toward the western horizon, they spotted two men in a raft. Abandoning the old plank, they made their way to the raft and climbed in. The other two survivors had found it a few hours earlier. On the inside it said, "USS *Johnston* DD 557." It must have blown overboard during the battle.

Inside they found a survival tin, which had biscuits, but also matches and cigarettes. They pulled out the cigarettes and began passing them around. While the third bit of rolled up tobacco made its way from man to man, a wave crashed into the raft and soaked the tin. No more matches, which meant no more cigarettes. The men wanted to cry.

Back in the main group the afternoon wore on into evening, and the men wondered who had won the battle. If they had won, why hadn't they been rescued by now?

More men began to drink saltwater. Pharmacist Mate Schmuff told them not to, but they did it anyway. Others were strung out on morphine. Some were too tired to care anymore.

The sharks returned, forcing the men to fight for their lives one more time. The exhausted men took turns kicking at the sharks. When they got really close, the sailors would bash the sharks on the nose with their fists.

A rainstorm passed overhead, providing a bit of relief. The men held out their hands and hats to collect a few mouthfuls of water.

As the night wore on, the men began to shiver and their teeth chattered. The warm tropical waters were 80 degrees, but human bodies are 98 degrees. The men were getting hypothermia. They huddled close for warmth. By the time the sun rose on the third day, many were just waiting for the end to come.

TIN CAN SAILORS SAVE THE DAY!

CHAPTER 14

Rescue

EARLY IN THE MORNING DUSTY POKED HIS HEAD UP. A dark shape came over the horizon. When it drew closer, he saw a flag that had red and white stripes with a blue patch in the corner.

"There's a ship!" he yelled.

It was a landing craft, a small rectangular ship designed for landing men on beaches.

It headed straight toward them. When finding sailors adrift at sea, the rescuers often tested the nationality of the sailors by asking a question that only Americans would know the answer.

When the vessel slowed to a stop, a crewman called out, "Who won the World Series?"

One of the survivors yelled back, "Who the hell cares? Get us out of here!"

The crewmen tossed nets over the side of the landing ship. Dusty grabbed hold of the net but couldn't pull himself up. An officer climbed down and helped him the

LCIs (Landing Craft Infantry) like this one picked up the *Johnston* survivors

rest of the way. When he reached the top and stood up, his legs wobbled, so he leaned on the officer.

Then Dusty got a little soup, and they carried him below deck, where there were some familiar faces. Other survivors from the *Johnston* were asleep on crates filled with blue colored rockets. Then the air raid warning sounded. Japanese planes were strafing the landing craft. The ship's 40mm antiaircraft guns filled the sky with rounds while empty shell casings popped out and rolled around the deck.

Dusty couldn't be bothered. With gunfire all around him, he lowered his head, closed his eyes, and slept.

Photo of men from the USS *Gambier Bay* being rescued during the Battle off Samar

TIN CAN SAILORS SAVE THE DAY!

Epilogue

B OB HAGEN, LIEUTENANT WELCH AND CLINT CARTER all survived as well. Chuck Campbell, the man who was "too salty for the sharks," lived to tell his tale.

These men were among the 145 survivors of the *Johnston* who returned to Leyte Gulf, where they were put aboard the hospital ship *Hollandia*. Captain Evans was not among them. He and 183 of the sailors gave their lives to protect the escort carriers and the landing fleet.

The Allied invasion was a success. By June the Philippines were back in American hands. The *Johnston's* gallant defense of the carriers and transport ships had played a big part in the success of the invasion. In August 1945, Japan surrendered.

The *Johnston* and its crew were showered with medals and praise. The *Johnston* received the Presidential Unit Citation from both the United States government and the Philippines government. President Roosevelt awarded the Medal of Honor to Captain Evans for his "indomitable courage and professional skill...in turning back the enemy."

Photo of the SS *Lurline* berthed in Hawaii, 1932

To Dusty Rhodes and the other survivors, though, they were just doing their jobs. Nonetheless, the men had earned a break. The *Hollandia* sailed to New Guinea, where the men were transferred to the S.S. *Lurline*, which took them to Australia and then headed for America.

On Thanksgiving Day the men had an outrageous meal aboard the *Lurline*: turkey, gravy, stuffing, beef Wellington, turtle soup, fruit cocktail, buttered vegetables, cranberry sauce, salad, olives, desert and coffee. It was an unbelievable meal for men who exactly one month earlier had been floating in the dark waters off Samar trying desperately not to become a shark's meal. They had plenty of time to digest the rich food as the *Lurline* sailed slowly across the Pacific. The trip took three weeks.

Early one morning the *Lurline* sailed under the Golden Gate Bridge and docked at Treasure Island. They

Captain Evans's widow and sons looking
at Congressional Medal of Honor

were back in America, but Dusty was not quite home. He
arrived in Kansas in time for Christmas. Sitting around
the dinner table with his family and Carol, Dusty could
imagine the years ahead, but his thoughts drifted to those
he left behind.

All of the emotions plowed into Dusty, and he knew
what he had to do. The man who had never thought much
about tomorrow took a deep look into the future and
knew that it had to include one person.

He took all of his money and headed to the jewelry
shop in town. He asked Carol to go for a walk, and when
they found a quiet place, he knelt to the ground and

pulled out a ring. "Carol, now I know life is short. Will you marry me?" Soon they were married. In time, they had three daughters.

Hagen, who was already married, came back to his wife and they started a family as well. Carter and Welch and the others followed suit. Life returned to normal, but it wasn't the same. The loss of their friends still stung, and they started getting together once a year to remember.

They began to wonder if others would remember as well, but who could forget the blazing shells and hungry sharks off Samar? From the first sharp turn toward the enemy to the last man climbing onto the rescue craft, the story has a life all its own. Like the beating of a huge heart, it echoes.

About the Author

KEVIN MCDONALD GREW UP IN NORTHERN CALIFORNIA, where he played baseball, canoed down the Russian River and read every book he could find about World War Two. He became intrigued by the danger and sacrifice that constantly confronted the men on the front lines. How did they get themselves to do it? How did they overcome the stress and fear?

After graduating from Carleton College in Minnesota with a degree in Asian studies, Kevin lived in Japan for several years. While living in Tokyo, Kevin studied the Japanese language, martial arts and Japanese history. Upon returning home to California, Kevin began teaching 5th grade. Kevin saw his students reading about Captain Underpants and vampires, and he wondered if he could tell the stories of real heroes—the Soldiers, Sailors, Marines and Airmen of the U.S. Armed Forces.

World War II was a natural place to start. The vast sweep of the conflict engulfed the entire world and included every kind of engagement possible. Kevin chose to write about the Battle of Leyte Gulf, which was the last great fleet action in history. One particular engagement off the coast of the Philippine island of Samar showed American heroism at its finest. His first book in the American Heroes series tells the story of that fateful day.

Acknowledgments

The author would like to thank the following sailors for providing interviews:

USS *Gambier Bay*
Owen Wheeler

USS *Hoel*
Bob DeSpain, Larry Morris,
John Oracz, Glenn Parkin

USS *Johnston*
Bill Allen, Bob Attebery, Bill Blarr,
Harold "Dusty" Rhodes, Clarence Trader

USS *Samuel B. Roberts*
Glenn Huffman

The author would like to thank the following individuals for providing interviews:

Ernest Evans Jr., son of Captain Evans
Beverly Stirling, widow of Lieutenant Elton Stirling

And thanks to Robert Jon Cox and *bosamar.com* for the use of maps in chapters 9-11.